Young
Joey
Koalakin

A Fun Day

Margaret Kamla Kumar
Laila Savolainen

U
ma
Publishing
Group

A catalogue record for this book is available from the National Library of Australia

NATIONAL LIBRARY OF AUSTRALIA

ISBN: 978-0-6454789-5-2 (hardback)
ISBN: 978-0-6454789-2-1 (paperback)
ISBN: 978-0-6454789-3-8 (ebook)

Author: Margaret Kamla Kumar
Illustrator: Laila Savolainen

Interior and Cover Layout: Pickawoowoo Author Services
Print and Channel Distribution: Lightning Source / Ingram (US/UK/AUS/ EUR)

Publisher: Uma Publishing Group
www.umapublishing.com

Dedication

This book is dedicated to all children who through their experiences of fun and play become aware of their natural environment.

Young Joey Koalakin, who was fondly referred to as Joey Koalakin, Young Joey or as Koalakin, climbed out of Mama Akashi's pouch and stretched himself. "What a glorious day this is," he said. "What a great sleep, Mama will be happy I got it all done in just 14 hours and not the normal 20 hours like everyone else does."

"Now for some fun," he said to himself. He clambered up the eucalyptus tree that was his family home and called out to the other koalas in the nearby trees. "Time to play," he said. But there was no response from any of his friends.

Young Joey Koalakin gathered that it was still 'sleep time 'for his friends. "Oh well, I'll just have some 'quiet time'," he mused. "'Quiet time' is just as important for little koalas as it is for big koalas."

So, Young Joey sat snugly between two branches on his family tree and began to dream.

"It's so great to be a joey. I'm still young enough to sleep in Mama's pouch, I don't have to do any chores and my job is to eat, sleep and play: day in and day out. This is the best koala haven; I can think of."

With these fun-filled thoughts, Young Joey Koalakin got up from his musings and thought he would become adventurous. He tried swinging from branch to branch with his tail the way he had seen some animal friends do.

But he fell.

He landed in the foliage at the base of the tree, with a soft thud. That made him laugh.

"Not to worry," he said to himself. "There are other ways I can do this."

This time, using his front paws, he began swinging over and under the branches.

"It worked!" he said with a satisfied squeal of delight.

Young Joey Koalakin began swinging in this way from branch to branch.

He then clambered to the tips of the branches and jumped to the next branch and from there to the next tree. "Is this really me!" he said to himself. "Oh, what fun to be had, if one puts their mind to it."

As he was doing this, Young Joey Koalakin noticed that his nose began to quiver. He realised that like his koala companions, his nose had gained in sensitivity. "Wow! My nose has achieved super koala powers. I have to find what it is that I am smelling. It's time for my nose to help me become stronger." He began to follow his nose.

This time, he began to walk steadily from one tree branch to the next. As he did so, he began to catch the scent of luscious eucalyptus leaves. To smell them more clearly, he slowed down. "Oh, so this is why Grandfather Kashy and Mama have this slow koala gait. They are looking for food for us," he said in surprise.

Young Joey Koalakin began to walk in the same way.

He began picking different varieties of eucalyptus leaves. After having collected a pawful of leaves, he seated himself comfortably in the wedge of a eucalyptus tree and began tasting the leaves he had collected.

He recognised the Blue Gum and Manna, but the other leaves were just as delicious.

Overcome with excitement , he said, "I have to show this to Mama." He put the leaves he had collected in his mouth the way he had seen Mama Akashi do when she was feeding him.

This time he did not clamber down backwards feet first but crawled down slowly with his front paws using them one after the other, all the while with the leaves in his mouth.

"What fun," he thought. "Mustn't forget this style!"

Having reached his Mother's favourite sitting spot, Young Joey Koalakin turned to her with excitement, exclaiming, "Look Mama, see what I found."

He showed her the leaves and began to explain what he had done, and how he had tasted a few of the leaves and recognised them but not the other ones.

Mama Akashi was equally excited. She saw that there was Blue Gum, Long-leaved Box and Brown Stringybark leaves, Manna Gum, River Red Gum and Swamp Gum. It was all food that they could eat, happily, for many days to come.

She clasped Young Joey to her furry chest and gave him a hug. "Oh, my Koalakin! You are a true koala now. You are not a koala bear, as I have heard the humans call us. But you must finish your sleep time, like your little koala friends, so that you are big and strong when you go out into the wide world."

In response, with a koala grunt, Young Joey Koalakin spread out his paws and sent a message out to the rest of the world. "Whoop, whoop whoopee, I am a koala: not a koala bear. Growing up is such fun!"

He then slid down into Mama Akashi's pouch and fell into a comfortable sleep. His fun day had turned out to be so glorious!

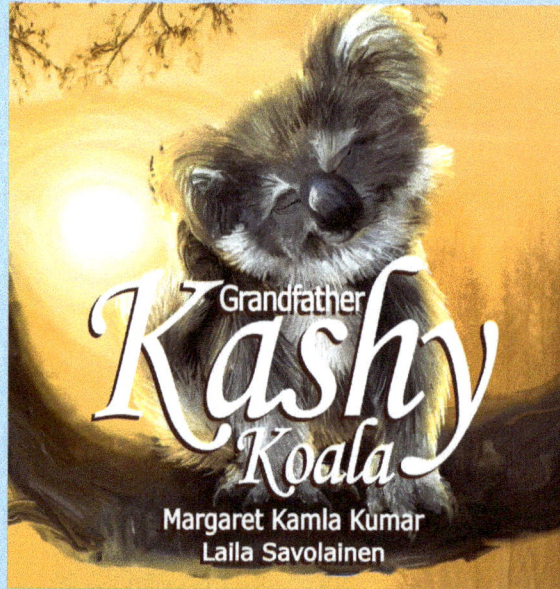

Grandfather
Kashy
Koala
Margaret Kamla Kumar
Laila Savolainen

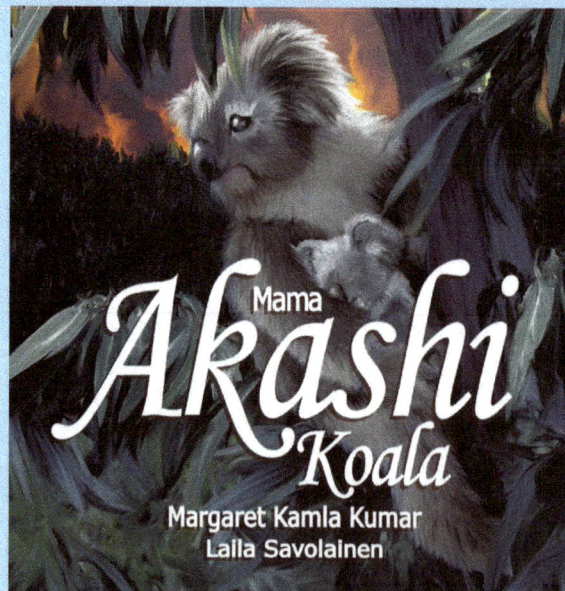

Mama
Akashi
Koala
Margaret Kamla Kumar
Laila Savolainen

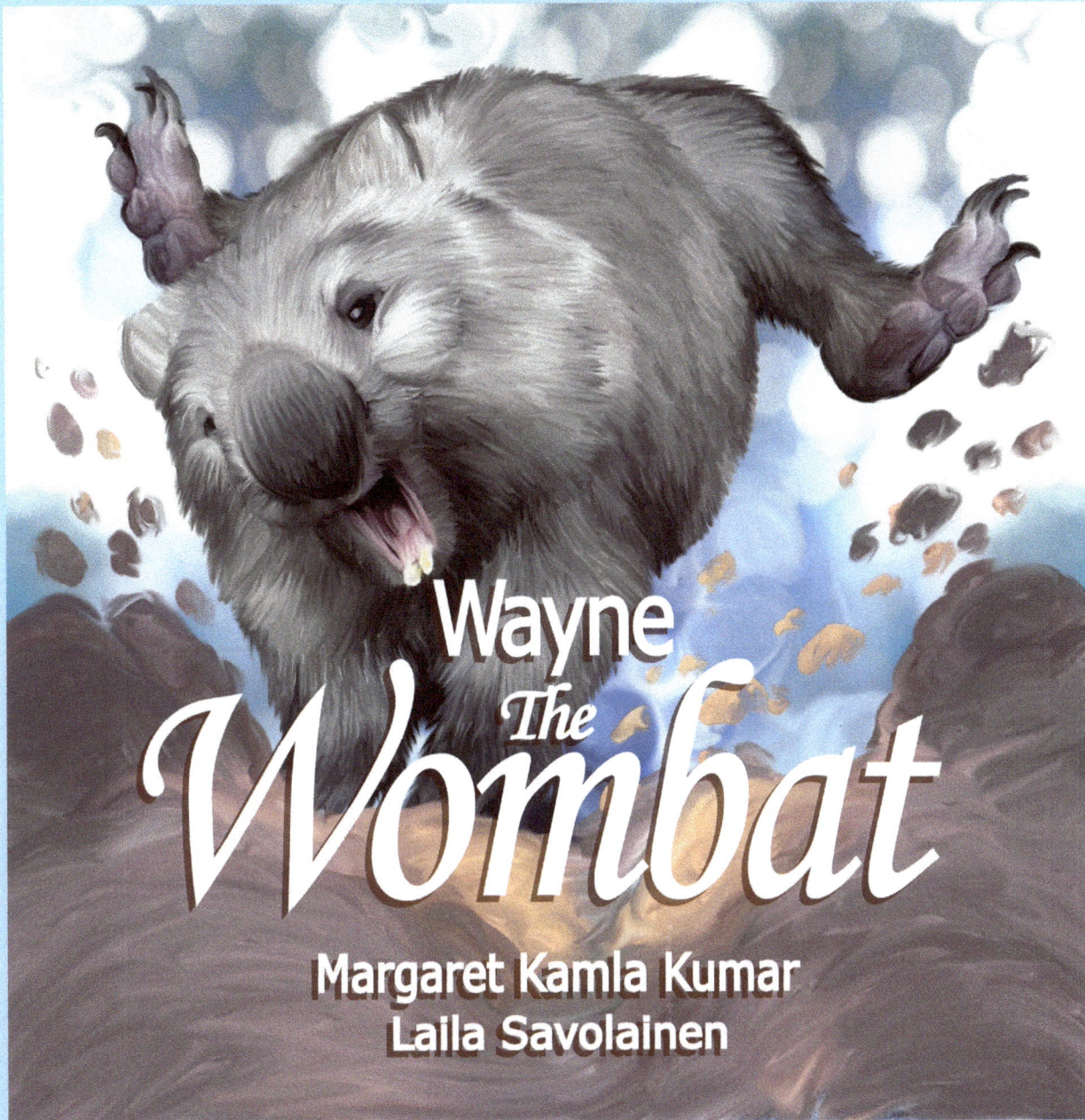

Wayne
The
Wombat

Margaret Kamla Kumar
Laila Savolainen

www.ingramcontent.com/pod-product-compliance
Lightning Source LLC
Chambersburg PA
CBHW051557030426
42334CB00034B/3474